# Third Time a Charm

Written by Kate Foster

Illustrated by Jacinta Read

**Collins**

# Chapter 1

The crowds cheered and clapped as gymnasts in colourful, patterned leotards, singlets and tracksuits stretched and prepared. The arena had turned into a rainbow of activity.

Competition day had arrived and Billie Nicks was as nervous as nervous could be – but she was also excited. Today, the boys' and girls' competitions were happening at the same time, so she had both of her best friends there – Gracie *and* Caleb.

Her squad was performing first on the floor. While the boys warmed up on the pommel horse, Billie helped her teammates, Freya, Jessica and Gracie, to rehearse at the edge of the blue sprung area.

They always helped one another perform and perfect moves, but when it came to entire routines, they relied on Billie for her brilliant memory. She knew everyone else's sequences as if they were hers.

Billie practised her own routine again. She was determined to stick all the landings on her tumbles, ensure her legs were straight in her leaps and put bucket-loads of expression into her dance moves.

Today, she'd brought her A game!

A squealing buzzer filled the arena. Panic whirled through Billie's body. She immediately pressed her hands to her ears and closed her eyes tightly until it stopped.

"Are you OK, Billie?" inquired Gracie. "Do you want your headphones?"

Billie's heartbeat slowed as the buzzer ended. She sighed, relieved, and shook her head.

Billie had hypersensitive hearing. Usually, she could predict and prepare for when loud sounds occurred in her day-to-day life and would wear her noise-cancelling headphones and squeeze her stress ball. But today, Billie's mind was preoccupied with the competition. Thank goodness Gracie was here.

The two friends jogged to join the others, and all four girls huddled together with their coach to review the schedule. Billie kept her eyes lowered, admiring all their neatly painted toenails – purple to match club colours.

Willow Creek Gymnastics Club ran weekly training sessions especially for neurodivergent children where the gymnasium was quiet and less busy than other sessions. Billie and Jessica were autistic, as was Caleb, and Gracie and Freya had ADHD. Billie, Gracie and Caleb had become best friends over the past five years.

"Right, Willow Warriors," Coach Maggie announced excitedly. "I know you're ready. We've trained hard for this day. No matter what happens, what goes right, or wrong, we're a team."

The girls nodded and smiled at each other. Gracie bounced on her toes and shook out her arms.

"So, we cheer, celebrate, support and most importantly – "

Billie, Gracie and Freya all finished Coach Maggie's sentence at the same time. "Have fun!" Jessica, who was non-speaking, signed the same words.

Beside them, the boys' squad, also huddled with their coach, whooped gently.

Then, all eight of the Willow Creek gymnasts formed one large circle and gave an air-high-ten in the middle, their palms not actually touching as some of the children were sensitive to touch, including Billie. No one thought it was weird or questioned it. It was another thing Billie loved about her club.

"Good luck," Caleb whispered to Billie. "You're going to be amazing."

Billie grinned at her friend. "Thanks, Caleb. You too."

The two squads separated.

Their first rotation was about to begin.

# Chapter 2

It was Billie's third competition. The previous two times, she'd gone home early. The unfamiliar location, the bright lights, the hundreds of people, not to mention the constant unexpected sounds, had roiled inside her, causing her pain and making it hard to breathe.

But this time, Coach Maggie had brought all the competitors to the arena earlier in the week so they could become familiar with the size and layout of the venue. It was one less surprise they had on competition day. Plus, with not only Gracie here but Caleb too, Billie felt prepared and determined not to let down her teammates.

This was it!

Gracie, Freya and Jessica had performed their
floor routines and Caleb had nailed his performance
on the pommel horse. Now they sat around Billie on
a row of chairs, relaxing. Billie liked to be tidy, orderly
and peaceful. Coach Maggie said these were some of
Billie's numerous strengths. Her quiet way allowed others
to feel safe in her company.

Even though Billie didn't always feel calm on
the inside, she liked helping her friends feel this way.

Some people thought silence was uncomfortable, but
Billie disagreed. There was no point in speaking when
there was nothing to say!

9

A new piece of floor music started to play, making Billie imagine cowboys on galloping horses, and a tall gymnast from a rival club, St Matilda's, charged straight into a sequence of flips and somersaults, landing perfectly.

*Wow!*

"Right, Billie," Coach Maggie called. "Ready?"

Billie nodded, stood and removed her tracksuit.

"You'll be brilliant," Gracie declared.

"Smash it!" Caleb gave Billie a beaming smile.

"I'll try," Billie replied, placing her folded tracksuit into her bag.

Jessica signed, "Good luck!" and Billie signed back, "Thank you."

All Willow Creek club members were encouraged to learn sign language.

Gracie and Caleb chanted, "Blue Billie!" over and over.

Blue Billie was Gracie's nickname for Billie, because her favourite colour was blue and she loved blueberries. Billie knew Gracie wasn't being mean; she had nicknames for everyone. Gracie was the best at making sure no one felt left out. Plus, Blue Billie was a fun thing to say.

The music stopped, and the St Matilda's gymnast presented to the judges. The crowd cheered and whooped.

Billie carefully navigated around the Willow Creek clutter to climb the stairs. She walked elegantly into position.

The floor was bouncy under foot and despite the swirls of nerves in her belly, Billie felt light and excited to perform.

The head judge, an older man wearing a smart hat, gestured for Billie to begin. She presented herself by lifting her arms above her head, and then got into her starting pose.

The crowd hushed, and Billie's music started with a building drumbeat. She was in the zone.

# Chapter 3

The music thumped and boomed, the rhythm reaching every part of Billie's body.

Her first tumble was high, and she bounced straight into a twisting straddle jump. She connected quickly into her second tumble: a series of flips finishing with a straight back somersault. Her landing was solid.

*Dance sequence time ...*

Billie exhaled, relaxing so she could become a graceful ballet dancer.

*Sashay sashay, split leap, spin.*

*Into cartwheel and ...*

*Double leg kick.*

She'd practised incredibly hard in training as well as picturing her routine in her head whenever she could. It was now playing out in real life like a dream come true.

She stepped into the corner and inhaled deeply.

*Final tumble time ...*

Billie lifted her chin and gritted her teeth.

*Round off, back flip, full twisting straight back.*

*Land, stretch, now finish.*

She rolled into a sitting position, placed one hand on her hip, and on the final drumbeat, looked up dramatically at the vast ceiling.

Her floor routine was over.

She'd done it!

A second of silence was followed by an eruption of applause. The noise was sudden, and Billie winced, but it wasn't as loud as the happiness in her brain or the thumping of her heart.

She'd dreamt of this.

She presented to the judges, then returned to her friends.

They all air-hugged and high-fived.

"Wow, Billie!" exclaimed Gracie as they all took a seat.

"Big wows," added Caleb.

Jessica signed, "Brilliant."

"Thanks." Billie smiled, putting on her tracksuit to keep warm.

Billie was the last to perform on the floor, and now all the gymnasts had to pack up and move to the next rotation. For Willow Creek girls that was the vault and for the boys' squad it was the rings.

"That's one of your best routines ever, Billie," Coach Maggie remarked. "I'm so proud."

Billie glowed inside. She couldn't believe Coach Maggie had said that.

The girls lined up, and Billie's mind replayed her floor routine again. Happiness and pride warmed her tummy.

Then the buzzer sounded, snapping Billie right out of her pleasant thoughts. She screwed up her face, a sharp icy feeling whipping through her body. She'd forgotten to put on her headphones – again.

But then the usher arrived to take her squad to the vault, so Billie pushed her discomfort away, took another deep breath, and marched onwards.

# Chapter 4

Though the vault was Gracie and Caleb's favourite apparatus, it was Billie's second-to-least favourite. She was more of an elegant gymnast than powerful and speedy like her best friends.

In fact, everything about the vault forced Billie's anxiety to the limit. The fast movement – gymnasts charging down the runway. The thuds – pounding on the springboard. So much that could go wrong – under- or over-rotating.

Billie's warm-up vaults had gone well. Not perfectly, but well enough for her to feel confident she might do OK.

This time she was second to perform from her squad.

Caleb waved to her, several metres away where he sat with the other boys beside the rings. She waved back, her tummy settling knowing he wasn't too far away.

"I'm so proud of you right now," announced Gracie, sitting next to Billie and kicking off her sliders.

"Why?" asked Billie, frowning at the mess on the floor. "I'm only sitting here."

Gracie laughed. "No, I don't mean what you're doing right this second." She rolled her eyes, but in a playful way that made Billie smile. "I mean, it's your third competition and you're being amazing."

"Thanks," Billie replied. "Still three rotations to go."

Gracie shrugged and grabbed a packet of glittery hair clips from the floor. She clipped two into her golden hair. "True, but one thing at a time."

Billie nodded.

"And remember to put on your headphones!"

"Gracie," called Coach Maggie, "you're up." She beckoned Gracie over to the steps.

18

"Wish me luck." Gracie tossed the hair clip packet to the floor, and as she stepped away, she almost tripped on one of her abandoned sliders.

Billie caught her breath, relieved Gracie hadn't fallen. "Good luck, Gracieful." That was Billie's nickname for Gracie.

Gracie grinned, and then skipped over to Coach Maggie. Caleb wished her luck as she passed.

In between watching Gracie's magnificent vaults and Caleb's rings routine where he swung smoothly and powerfully, Billie helped Jessica and Freya practise. Then she moved to a tidier area to get in the zone. She pictured perfect vaults in her mind.

Knowing Gracie and Caleb were proud of her made Billie feel sparkly and boosted her to do her very best.

With air-high-fives to the others and a wave to Caleb, Billie stood at the end of the runway, trying to block out the yelling crowd, electric guitar music of a floor routine and all the people walking and talking around her.

Things were getting louder; she was sure of it.

With more deep breaths, she presented to the judges and pointed her toe forwards.

*You've got this, Billie ...*

And she sprinted.

*Thrust off the horse, tight tuck, bend your legs, absorb the landing.*

Billie's feet hit the mat with a thump, and she took two small steps forward. Not brilliant, but it could have been worse.

Thankfully, her second vault went better. She only had to shuffle her feet slightly to balance.

With a sigh of relief, Billie wove back around Gracie and Jessica's clothes. She rubbed her ears.

"Need your headphones?" Freya asked.

Billie heard Freya's question, but it didn't seem to make any sense in her mind. She frowned, staring down at her bag between her bare feet, and continued to massage her ears.

She glanced sideways, towards Caleb, hoping to get his attention. He was busy cheering on his teammate.

Beside Billie, Jessica and Gracie ate bananas. The sounds of their chewing and the banana smell made Billie's skin prickle and her tummy squirm. So, she decided to follow Freya, who was heading to their next rotation, instead.

# Chapter 5

The Willow Creek gymnasts were now onto their third rotation, and it was Billie's turn to perform her bar routine – the hardest and trickiest of them all.

She checked that her hair clips were securing any loose strands from her neat ponytail and peeked at her friends. Caleb and Gracie stood side by side, Caleb smiling and Gracie bouncing on the spot.

*They believe in me.*

She needed to believe in herself, too.

She lifted both of her arms straight above her head and smiled at the three smartly dressed judges sitting side by side next to the uneven bars.

23

Billie pointed one toe forwards, then stared at the chalky low bar. She blew out a long breath to settle the nerves swarming about inside her and block out the sounds.

She jumped, catching the bar in a puff of white, and swung into her first moves.

*Legs stretched, toes pointed, arms and hands relaxed.*

She nailed her handstands *and* her full pirouette.

But then she lost her focus, and hesitated.

*It's OK. Relax.*

She added two extra swings to give her memory time to catch up.

Coach Maggie wouldn't be happy, and Billie would lose marks.

Billie squatted, curling her toes over the low bar.

*Push off, catch the high bar and kick.*

Billie gained momentum.

*Just the dismount left.*

She had to get this right.

Billie fixed her eyes on her hands grasping the springy bar. She then placed her toes on the bar between her hands.

*Here we go ...*

Billie gritted her teeth with determination.

*Kick, feet first, shoulders follow* ...

She tucked into her somersault.

*Now!*

She kicked into a half turn and spotted the mat. Her shoulders dipped, and the music of a floor routine exploded with a crashing cymbal, bursting into her ears and brain.

*No!*

*Must concentrate!*

Eyes on the mat below, she landed, knees bending to absorb the impact. Billie took a step forward to balance herself. She joined her feet back together, raised her arms and presented to the judges.

It hadn't gone well, but ...

Billie had completed three of her routines.

*THREE!*

This was the furthest she'd ever come, and her heart pounded faster than the violins playing in the arena.

Only one more rotation left, and it was her favourite apparatus – the beam.

She needed to remain steadfast.

She could do this.

*Can I?*

Her fast-beating heart and short breaths made her unsure.

# Chapter 6

Billie wrung her hands and wandered back to Caleb and Gracie, but she accidentally kicked Jessica's water bottle and stumbled. Alarm and fear fluttered in her chest.

"Blue Billie, yay!" her friends chanted.

Billie couldn't smile. Inside her was a jumble of emotions. She wished her friends weren't so messy and would stop giving her attention. She needed to sit, alone, and listen to her thoughts.

She grimaced. Her chest twinged and tightened.

"Great job, superstar!" Coach Maggie said. "Your turn, Gracie."

As Coach Maggie and Gracie headed to the bar, Caleb squatted beside Billie, spinning the fidget ring on his middle finger.

29

"I did all those extra swings," Billie whispered, her voice wobbly.

Caleb carried on spinning, silently.

Billie sighed, her hands and fingers shaking and odd feelings still flittering in her chest.

Caleb shrugged, his eyes fixed on his ring. "You covered it up well and completed the routine. That's what matters."

Billie's mind jumped to another worry. "I didn't say good luck to Gracie."

"Gracie knows you're thinking it."

Billie didn't reply; her brain was filling up with too much information.

She looked past Caleb. Her bag was the only one on a chair and zipped up, her black sliders neatly underneath. Everywhere else was super messy and disorganised, clothes, equipment, tape and hair clips scattered everywhere.

She'd tried hard to understand that her teammates always knew where everything was in the chaos of their belongings. She couldn't always accept it, though.

Caleb stood. "I need to prepare for the vault now. I'll be back soon."

Billie watched Caleb's bare feet dash away, but his departure made her heart beat extra fast. She gasped, trying to draw enough air into every part of her lungs. Her clothes were feeling tight, and she was suddenly very hot.

Maybe a drink would help. Billie unzipped her bag and gulped water from her purple bottle, but her thoughts remained as messy as the floor around her. She wanted to tidy up, but her friends wouldn't like that.

Freya was preparing to perform her bar routine after Gracie, swinging her arms side to side and up and down. Billie longed to go over and help her, to cheer on her friends, but she couldn't.

Jessica plopped down noisily on the seat next to Billie.

Billie's stomach twirled.

Jessica's black bun glistened under the arena's lights. The lights were so bright and intense.

Jessica flapped her hands and then signed something, but it was too fast for Billie to understand.

Nausea growled in her tummy.

Movements blurred, her vision zooming in and out of focus, catching gymnast's bare feet and coaches' trainers walking this way and that. It was if someone had hit fast forward on the world around her.

She startled as Gracie and Jessica sprung to their feet, air-clapping as Freya performed her moves.

*Can't breathe.*

Music of another floor routine started, instruments playing rapid melodies.

*Need to breathe.*

The crowd's yells grew louder.

*Make it stop.*

There were too many colours. Too much activity.

*I need to leave!*

33

An enormous, uncomfortable lump lodged in Billie's chest. She squeezed her eyes tightly closed. She wanted to scream, to run far away.

Gentle voices seeped into Billie's ears, one gradually becoming clearer.

*Caleb.*

Then another.

*Gracie.*

She opened one eye.

A tear, then another, trickled and dripped from Billie's eyes.

*I want to go home.*

# Chapter 7

Billie opened her mouth to speak, but no words came. Instead, she gripped more tightly to her thighs.

"Do you want your headphones, Billie?" Gracie asked, crouching down in front of her.

Billie's words remained stuck somewhere inside her. She watched Caleb's hand reach for her bag, and then Gracie's, who pulled out her strawberry-shaped stress ball.

Caleb placed Billie's fluffy blue headphones securely over her ears. The arena noises muffled immediately, reducing to a low murmur. With shaking, almost numb hands, she took the strawberry from Gracie and squished it in her palms, passing it from one hand to the other.

*One, two, three ...*

She passed it to the other hand.

*One, two, three ...*

She passed it back.

The repetitive squeezing helped her mind order her thoughts.

Gradually, the tightness in her chest lessened, enough for her to lean back in the chair.

Her friends stood around her, like a protective wall, and she closed her eyes again. She breathed in and out, squishing her strawberry, until she felt a light tapping on the side of her chair.

Billie opened one eye to see Coach Maggie's soft wrinkled face, and her kind, warm smile. Coach Maggie gestured behind her, and Billie peeked quickly at the commotion of gymnasts and coaches collecting their bags, and ushers dressed in black arriving with clipboards to lead everyone to their final rotation.

*The beam.*

Could Billie do it? Could she perform?

She focused on her teammates, even Caleb who hadn't yet left her side to rejoin his squad. Freya and Jessica grabbed tracksuits, sliders, tape, water bottles and any other remaining belongings from the floor and chairs.

Finally, Billie's legs worked, and she stood. She shoved her strawberry into her pocket and wiggled her feet into her sliders. She joined the line and Caleb signed goodbye to her before scurrying off.

Freya led the way, Jessica next, then Gracie and Billie at the back – the same as always. Familiar, predictable, safe. They paraded towards the beam, their footsteps in time with each other.

Billie was aware of all the hustle and bustle around her as gymnasts scampered here and there. Stewards collected score sheets, cleaned up apparatus and dragged springboards and mats around. Judges stood and stretched.

It hadn't bothered Billie earlier, but now it all seemed so hectic.

Billie's eyes trailed over the thin beige beam but something felt wrong. The lump in her chest was back, expanding.

Her brain had gone blank.

*Oh no.*

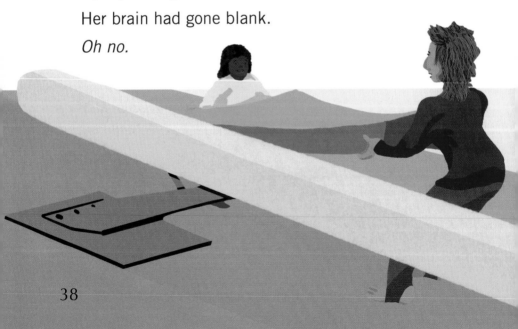

What was happening?

*Oh no no no.*

She couldn't remember how her routine even started.

Billie had been training extra days for weeks in the gym, as well as at home and in the playground at school.

*Why can't I remember my routine? What am I going to do?*

This was a disaster.

Tears pooled in her eyes again, and then she bumped into Gracie's back, not realising everyone had stopped walking.

# Chapter 8

Billie cried out at the sudden touch, and Gracie
spun around.

"I need to go home," Billie whimpered. Her eyes
blurred with more tears. "I need to go home," she
repeated, imploring. "I need Caleb."

Things had been going so well. Yet she was about to
leave another competition without finishing it.

Billie's teammates surrounded her again. Her bag
was peeled from her shoulder, and she was guided to
a nearby seat. Coach Maggie stood in front of her, her
fingers with painted purple nails pressed to her chest.
Billie watched as Coach Maggie inhaled and exhaled, her
chest expanding.

Billie's breaths shuddered, but she stared hard at Coach Maggie's movements and copied.

*In and out.*

Gradually, she got her breathing under control.

*In and out.*

The tears subsided, but anxiety continued to thrash in her belly and tighten her throat.

*In and out.*

Billie eyed the others warming up, but Coach Maggie remained still and breathing deeply. She pointed at Billie's ears, and Billie lifted one of her headphones.

"Can you tell me how you're feeling?" she asked, her voice gentle.

Billie glanced at the beam. "I want to go home," Billie pleaded.

Coach Maggie nodded. "OK. What else?"

"It's too loud and hot and busy in here," Billie whispered.

"Good. Anything else?" Coach Maggie coaxed, one more time.

"I can't remember my routine," Billie cried. Saying the words aloud made her feel dizzy, her head and heart overflowing with a big swirling mass of emotion.

Coach Maggie nodded again. "Let's see if we can fix that."

Gracie and Caleb appeared beside Coach Maggie.

"Do you want to go somewhere quiet?" Caleb asked.

Billie inhaled deeply. "Yes ... please."

Caleb and Gracie smiled.

"Come on then, Blue Billie, let's go."

# Chapter 9

Billie's legs were unsteady, but with an encouraging nod from Coach Maggie, she followed her friends.

Caleb and Gracie weaved Billie through stretching, chatting gymnasts from other clubs and headed towards an exit at the side of the arena. Billie kept her head down. Double doors swung shut and the busy bustling activity of the arena was no longer visible.

Peace enveloped Billie, wrapping her in a tranquil embrace. Sounds disappeared completely and the quiet corridor healed her. She lifted one of her headphones.

"Are you feeling better?" Caleb asked, spinning his ring.

Billie concentrated on her body. She felt less flustered out here, away from the commotion of the competition. She nodded.

"Good. Now it's our turn to become you, Blue Billie."
Gracie's blue eyes glistened, and her freckled
cheeks flushed.

Billie frowned. What did Gracie mean?

"You're always there when we forget our
routines, right?"

Billie nodded. She loved helping the others.

"Well, now we're here to help you remember yours,"
Caleb announced.

A smile crept onto Billie's face.

"Headphones off and let's get started!"
Gracie declared.

Billie did as she
was told, placing
her headphones
and strawberry to
the side.

"Ready?"
Caleb asked.

"Yup," Billie
replied, pleased
she'd found her
voice again.

44

Pointing toes on the shiny floor, they got to work.

First, Billie watched Gracie run through Billie's entire routine – without the acrobatics – using a taped line on the floor as the beam. She spoke aloud the whole time, naming each of the moves as she performed them.

Next, Billie watched Gracie perform it again. This time, Caleb chose a different taped line beside Gracie's, and copied everything Gracie did.

Billie placed her hand over her mouth and giggled.

Gracie added wild flourishes here and there with her hands, wiggling and making cheeky expressions at Billie.

Caleb tried to keep up, but often made up his own moves.

Finally, Billie took over from Caleb, using his line, and side by side, she and Gracie executed her routine twice more.

Caleb glanced at his watch. "I have to warm up for the horizontal bar. Will you be OK?"

Filled with warmth and love for her best friend, Billie approached him and smiled. "Yes, thank you. Good luck!" She held out one hand and Caleb air-high-fived it, then he disappeared back through the double doors.

"Are you sure you'll be OK?" Gracie asked, lovingly.

Billie turned to her other best friend and nodded. "As long as you and Caleb are here, I'm ready."

# Chapter 10

Billie rolled her ankles, first left and then right, and then she rolled her wrists. She rose onto tiptoes then lowered back down.

"You have sooooo got this," affirmed Freya.

"You're brilliant," signed Jessica.

"Of course she is," Gracie said and signed. "Billie is about to perform a gold medal-winning beam routine. Right?"

Billie grinned. "Right!"

"You're always there when your teammates need you, Billie," Coach Maggie added. "But you must always remember that they're here for you, too."

Billie did know. She was lucky to have such understanding and caring friends by her side.

Just then, Caleb jogged over. "Did I make it in time?"

"You sure did," Gracie replied.

Still nervous and unsure, Billie climbed the steps to the beam area. She was ready to perform her final piece.

One of the judges gestured to Billie that they were ready, and Billie strode to the springboard placed by the beam. She rubbed her sweaty hands together and rolled her ankles one more time. Her heart pounded as adrenaline rushed through her.

She looked to her friends once more, all of them smiling and air-clapping.

With one final steadying breath, Billie blocked out the floor music behind her, the crowd in front and the expectant faces of the judges sitting on the other side of the beam. She was in control. All she had to do was finish this routine and she'd done it: she'd completed her first-ever competition.

One of the judges, a woman with grey hair and gold glasses and chain, raised her hand to Billie and she presented herself.

*Here we go …*

Feet together on the springboard, Billie placed her hands onto the beam, shoulder-width apart, bent her legs and bounced once. She whipped her feet over the beam.

*Head up, eyes down, now slowly, carefully.*

Billie raised her legs up and joined them in a handstand.

*Hold for three, two, one ...*

She cartwheeled out and stood tall on the beam.

*First move done.*

Billie flicked her hands and arms, stretched and flexed her toes and twisted her body in a sequence of dance moves that took her to the other end of the beam.

*Line it up.*

Billie placed one hand on top of the other and stared past them to the other end of the beam.

*Acrobatics time.*

*Ready.*

She kicked off.

*Cartwheel, back flip, whip.*

*Stick the landing ...*

Her shoulder dipped slightly on the landing, but she gritted her teeth and corrected herself, raising her arms to complete it.

*Second move done.*

Billie was completely in the zone, her hyperfocus back.

*Leap time.*

Light on her toes, Billie sprang forward.

*Split change, pike jump, tuck with half twist.*

*Yes!*

Billie inhaled and prepared for the move she found the hardest of all. She breathed out through her mouth.

*Up onto your toes, and full spin.*

*Stick it!*

She wobbled slightly but fought back, hard.

She didn't fall off. Phew.

*It's dismount time.*

This was it. The dismount was all that remained between Billie and victory.

It had never been about winning, receiving a medal, or standing on the podium. It was about making it through to the very end.

With a step and a skip, Billie launched high into her double twisting dismount.

*Stick the landing …*

*Perfection!*

She turned and presented to the judges, with a toothy smile plastered on her face as the crowds cheered. Before she'd even had a chance to put her arms down, Coach Maggie, Freya, Jessica and her best friends in the whole wide world, Gracie and Caleb, charged up the steps. In a circle of purple, they all bounced up and down.

Billie had done it!

She had never felt this happy.

As they filed back down to the seating area, Billie turned to Gracie and Caleb. "I couldn't have done this without you. Thank you."

Caleb shrugged and spun his ring. "Anything for you."

Gracie wiped a tear from her eye. "What he said."

The three of them sat in a line and smiled

at each other, Billie the biggest of all.

# Billie's competition diary

Dear diary,

Today was an amazing day – I finished my first gymnastics competition ever!

My floor routine went great! I felt **prepared** and **focused**.

The vault has never been my favourite, so I was **anxious**. But I was **relieved** with my performance (and to get it over with!).

# Ideas for reading

Written by Gill Matthews
*Primary Literacy Consultant*

**Reading objectives:**

- check that the text makes sense to them, discussing their understanding and exploring the meaning of words in context
- ask questions to improve their understanding
- predict what might happen from details stated and implied

**Spoken language objectives:**

- ask relevant questions to extend their understanding and knowledge
- use relevant strategies to build their vocabulary
- articulate and justify answers, arguments and opinions

**Curriculum links:** Relationships education – Respectful relationships

**Interest words:** prepared, focused, anxious, relieved, determined, grateful, proud

## Build a context for reading

- Ask children to look at the front cover of the book and to read the title. Discuss what the title means to them.
- Read the back-cover blurb. Explore children's responses and encourage them to predict what might happen in the story.
- Ask children what they know about gymnastics and competitions. Explore how children think performing in a gymnastics competition might make someone feel anxious.

## Understand and apply reading strategies

- Ask children to read pp2–12. Discuss the characters they have met in these chapters and what they are like.
- Ask how they think Willow Creek Gymnastics Club helps neurodivergent children like Billie.

My bar routine was the most demanding of them all. I lost focus for a moment, but I was **determined** and managed to get through it.

I felt overwhelmed before my turn on the beam — it was all too much. I was **grateful** for my understanding friends, who took the time to help me.

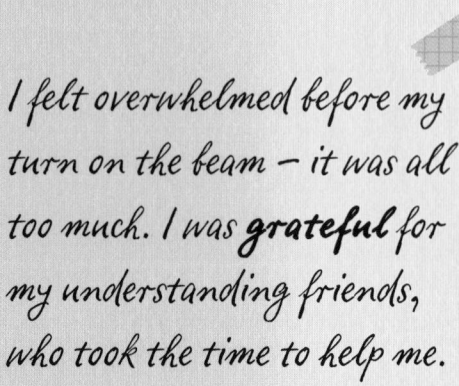

With their support, I did it!

I'm so **proud** of myself. ♡

♡ ✱